What Grows in My Garden

Apples Grow on Trees

Anne Rooney

Editor: Alexandra Koken
Designer: Melissa Alaverdy
Educational consultants:
   Jillian Harker and
   Heather Adamson

Copyright © QED Publishing 2013

First published in the UK in 2013
by QED Publishing
A Quarto Group Company
230 City Road,
London EC1V 2TT

www.qed-publishing.co.uk

ISBN 978 1 78171 207 8

A catalogue record
for this book is
available from
the British Library

Printed in China

Picture credits
(t=top, b=bottom, l=left, r=right,
c=centre, fc=front cover)
Alamy: 17b foodfolio
Dreamstime: 2-3 Inga Nielssen, 8
Elena Elisseeva, 10 fl orafau, 12 Piritia,
16 tl Marek Uliasz, 16tr Dolos 72,
16 Valentinar, 16 Petrp, 16 Jlvdream,
17tr Paulrommer, 17 Stargatech, 22
Asterixus, 23 Denisnata
FLPA: 9 Nigel Cattlin, 11 Kurt Moebus,
18 Erica Olsen
Getty: 14 Cultura/Axel Bernstoff, 19
Nigel Cattlin
Istock: 23c travellinglight
Shutterstock: 1 Elena Elisseeva, 2
Peter Zijlstra, 4 Mazzur, 5 Kirsanov, 6
Maks Narodenko, 7 Inga Nielsen, 8b
Kanusommer, 15 Z-art, 15b Smit, 16
br Kletr, 17tl Samokhin, 20-21 Andy
Dean Photography

Words in **bold**
can be found in
the Glossary on
page 24.

Contents

What is an apple?

Apples are firm fruits. They grow on trees.

Lots of apples grow on each tree every year. Apples hang from the tree by their **stems**.

stems

Growing the tree

An apple tree takes a long time to grow. It grows from a **seed**.

Seed

It takes a few years before a tree begins to grow apples.

Growing apples

The apple tree grows flowers in spring.

Bees take **pollen** between the flowers.

pollen

bee

Then the flower dies.
An apple starts to grow
behind the dead flower.
The apple grows larger
over summer.

dead
flower

Growing up

An apple tree needs water and sunlight to grow. It needs bees to visit the flowers.

Spring **frosts** can
kill the flowers.
Then there will be
no apples that year.

Ready to eat

Large, ripe apples are
easy to pick.

The stem is easy to snap when the apple is ripe.

stem

Pick the apple by twisting it.

13

Growing your own

It is easy to grow apple trees in the garden. Farmers grow apple trees in large orchards.

Some insects lay eggs on young apples. The eggs hatch into **maggots**. They feed on the apples.

maggot

Shapes and sizes

Apples can be big or small. They can be red, yellow, green or a mix of colours.

sweet

Some apples are sweet.

We eat these raw.

Some apples are sour.

We cook these.

sour

17

More apples one day

Unpicked apples fall to the ground. Animals eat some of these apples. Some apples will rot.

The apple seeds fall on the soil. They grow into new apple trees.

Good for you

Apples taste good. They make a healthy snack. Apples give us **vitamins**, **fibre**, sugar and water. Apples can help to keep us well.

There is a saying, "An apple a day keeps the doctor away!"

Tasty!

We eat most apples raw. Cooking apples are used to make apple pie, crisps, cake and other goodies.

apple sauce

apple pie

Apple sauce is another sweet treat.

apple juice

Apple juice tastes good.

Glossary

bee a flying insect that collects pollen

fibre part of a fruit that helps other food to move through the digestive system

frost a time of cold weather when the temperature drops below freezing

maggot the wormlike larval stage of some insects, such as flies

pollen tiny, yellow grains produced by flowers, needed to fertilize plants

seed part of a flowering plant from which a new plant grows

soil the top layer of earth, where plants grow

stem the stiff, sticklike part of some fruits that holds the apple to the tree

vitamin one of the nutritious parts of food that keeps bodies healthy